Text and illustrations copyright © 2023 by Izabela Ciesinska.
All rights reserved.

Published by Ascension Publishing Group, LLC.

With the exception of short excerpts used in articles and critical reviews, no part of this work may be reproduced, transmitted, or stored in any form whatsoever, printed or electronic, without the prior written permission of the publisher.

Scripture passages are from the Revised Standard Version–Second Catholic Edition © 2006 by the Division of Christian Education of the National Council of the Churches of Christ in the United States of America. Used by permission. All rights reserved.

Ascension
PO Box 1990
West Chester, PA 19380
1-800-376-0520
ascensionpress.com

Cover design by James Kegley

Photo credits: Page 30: Main image: AdobeStock/ DragoNika; Inset: Shutterstock/ Sabine Hagedorn

Printed in the United States of America

23 24 25 26 27 6 5 4 3 2 1

ISBN 978-1-954882-29-4

The Little Donkey and God's Big Plan

written & illustrated by
Izabela Ciesinska

West Chester, Pennsylvania

To George, one of my favorite people, ever.

To my mother, Irena, who is always praying for us.

And to all the young readers who
are eager to discover their purpose.

Many years ago, in a small, poor town near Bethany, there lived a little donkey. He was very excited about the world, and he had BIG dreams for his life!

He wanted to be as strong as an ox ...

as useful as a camel ...

and as graceful as a horse.

But he could be none of those things, because he was tied to a post, by the fence, near the house. Sometimes he would reach for people, trying to help them, but they didn't give him a chance.

Then one day, the little donkey was visited by a wonderful surprise ...

And she brought treats!

And she gave him something he never had before: scratches!

Every day, she untied him and took him for a walk. But it was only a little walk, in a circle.

The little donkey wanted to go farther and to do more, but before he knew it, they ended up back at the same post, by the same fence, near the same house.

"Someday you will go places and do wonderful things," the friendly girl told him. "God has a very special purpose for you."

The little donkey listened and wondered, *Did God have a plan for him?*

One sunny morning, instead of going in a circle, the friendly girl and the little donkey headed for the big market in the middle of the town. Up ahead, he could already see the bright tents and the baskets of food. The little donkey bucked with excitement. Maybe now he could pull a big cart or carry a heavy basket! Maybe this was his very special purpose!

But they had not gone very far when the little donkey's owner came running out of the house after them. He snatched the rope and shook his finger at the girl. "He's too young to go to the market," the man said.

And once again, he tied the little donkey back to the post.

The little donkey's ears drooped, and his head hung low.
But the friendly girl put her arms around his neck and whispered,
"Keep faith, little friend.
God has a plan for you."

The little donkey listened,
and despite his sadness, he got ready.

He did his exercises.

He ate all his meals so he would grow strong.

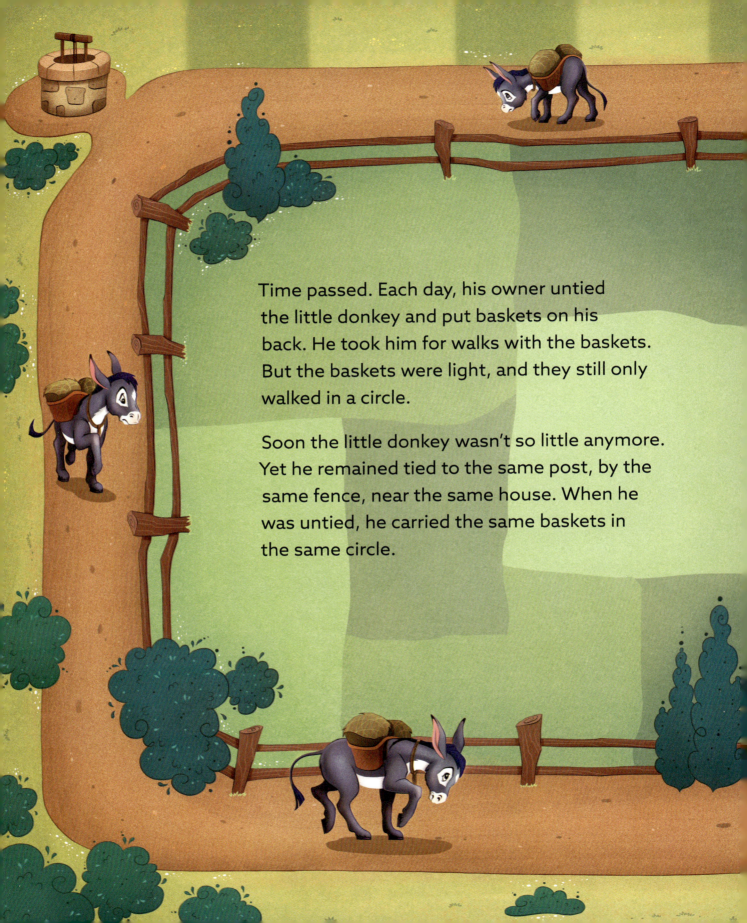

Time passed. Each day, his owner untied the little donkey and put baskets on his back. He took him for walks with the baskets. But the baskets were light, and they still only walked in a circle.

Soon the little donkey wasn't so little anymore. Yet he remained tied to the same post, by the same fence, near the same house. When he was untied, he carried the same baskets in the same circle.

The little donkey began to grow restless. But he remembered what his friend had told him—God had a very special purpose for him.

He kept faith in that promise, and he continued to carry those baskets in a circle as best he could.

One day, two men came to his owner's house and began to untie the little donkey. The friendly girl ran over to them. "Why are you untying him?" she asked the men.

"He is needed," the men told her, smiling.

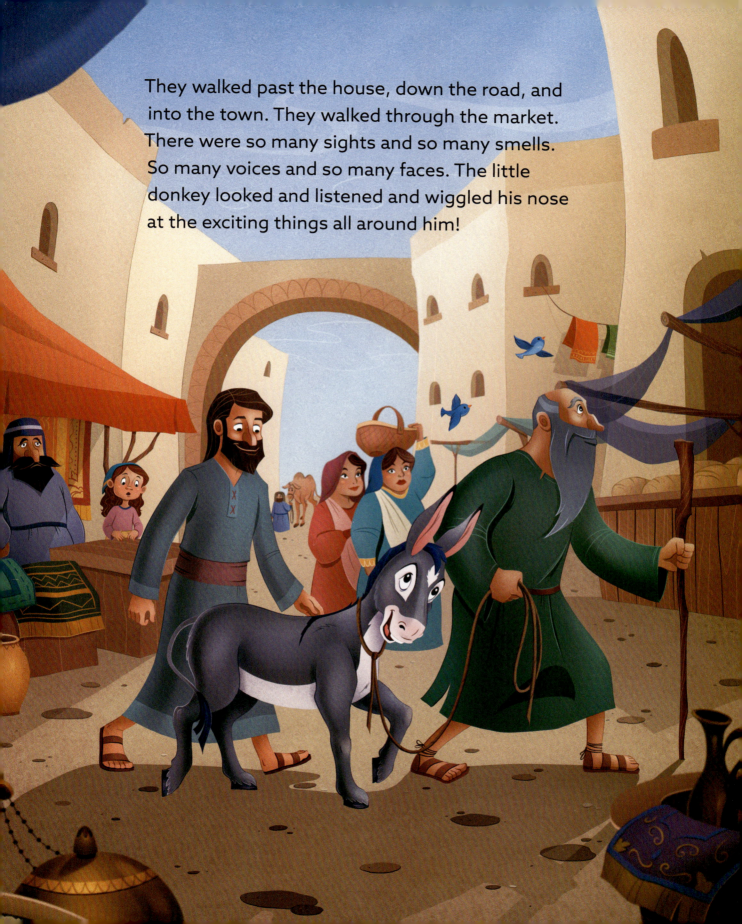

They walked past the house, down the road, and into the town. They walked through the market. There were so many sights and so many smells. So many voices and so many faces. The little donkey looked and listened and wiggled his nose at the exciting things all around him!

He walked with the men to a humble house. There were people outside, and one of them turned around and smiled at the little donkey.

"We meet at last, little one," the kind man said warmly.

Then he scratched the little donkey on the chin. The little donkey stretched his neck with delight.

"May I ride on your back?" the kind man asked.

The little donkey nodded his head in excitement.

He was glad he had practiced so long by carrying so many baskets. He was ready to carry this kind man.

Away they rode from the humble house, out of the small town, to a big city where a crowd of people greeted them. Some of them cheered for the kind man, and some of them even called him a "king."

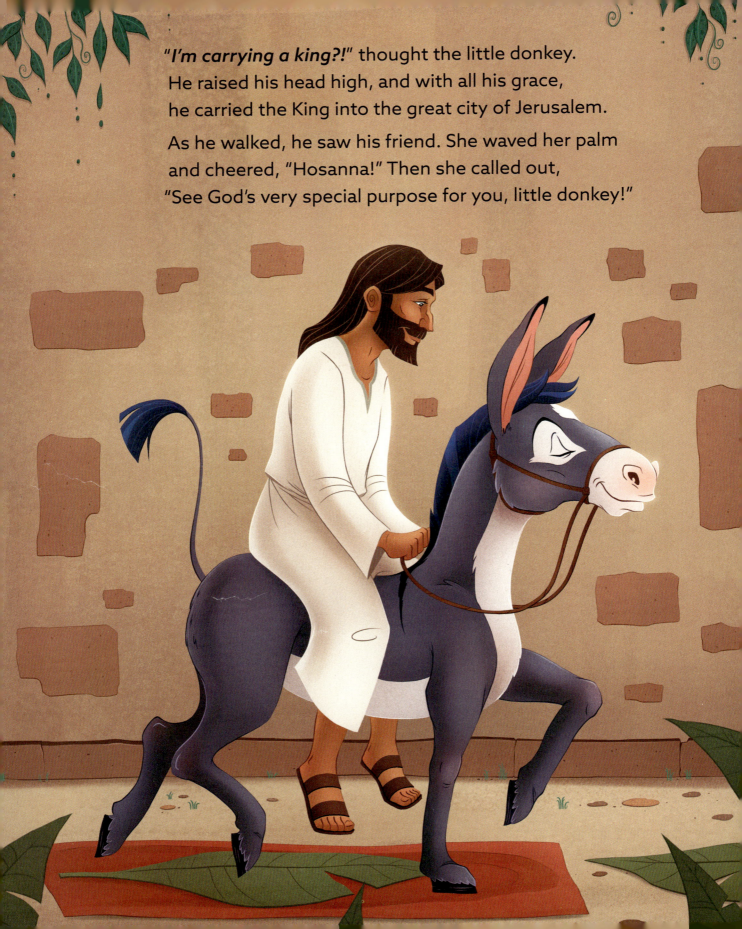

"I'm carrying a king?!" thought the little donkey. He raised his head high, and with all his grace, he carried the King into the great city of Jerusalem.

As he walked, he saw his friend. She waved her palm and cheered, "Hosanna!" Then she called out, "See God's very special purpose for you, little donkey!"

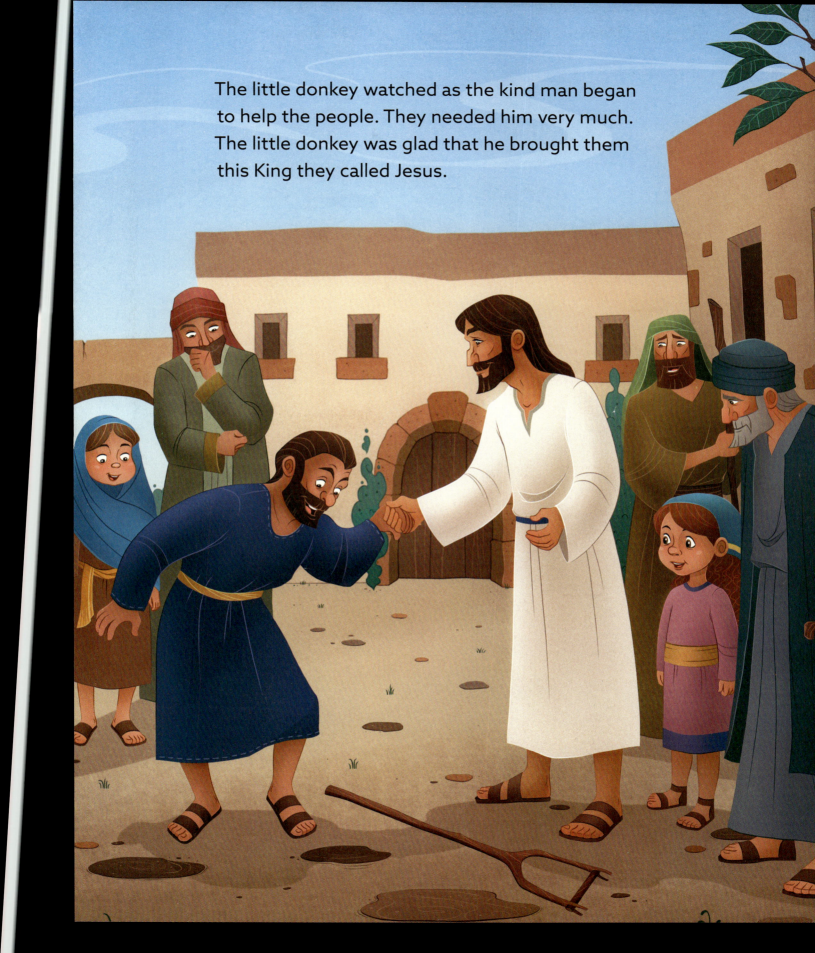

The little donkey watched as the kind man began to help the people. They needed him very much. The little donkey was glad that he brought them this King they called Jesus.

Jesus turned to the little donkey, looked into his eyes, and smiled warmly. "Thank you, little one," he said. "You kept faith and prepared yourself well even though you didn't know what would happen. Your service to me will be remembered for all time."

What is a Jerusalem Donkey?

"Rejoice greatly, O daughter of Zion! Shout aloud, O daughter of Jerusalem! Behold, your king is coming to you; righteous and having salvation is he, humble and mounted on a donkey, on a colt, the foal of a donkey."

—Zechariah 9:9

When the people of Jerusalem saw Jesus riding into town on a donkey, they recognized he was fulfilling the Old Testament prophecy of Zechariah about the arrival of Israel's king. Choosing a donkey showed Jesus is a different kind of king. A conquering king would have ridden into town on a horse. Instead, Jesus chose a donkey to demonstrate he is a humble king of peace.

It is likely that Jesus rode into Jerusalem on a Nubian donkey. While most donkeys have a dark stripe down their backs from their manes to their tails, Nubian donkeys also have a stripe across their shoulders. Many believe that these markings—which make the shape of a cross—are a fitting symbol of the special purpose the humble donkey served on Palm Sunday.

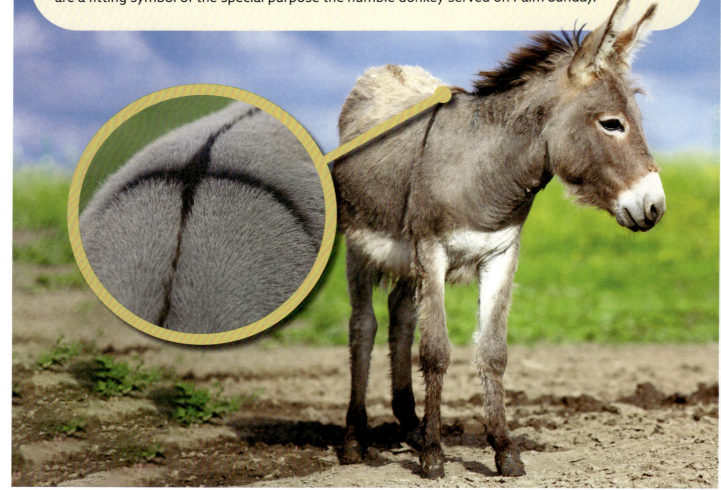